I
AM
SMOKE

Written by
Henry Herz

Illustrated by
Mercè López

TILBURY HOUSE PUBLISHERS

I am smoke.

I twirl in dark dance from every campfire.

Flickering flames work their mysterious magic on burning branches.

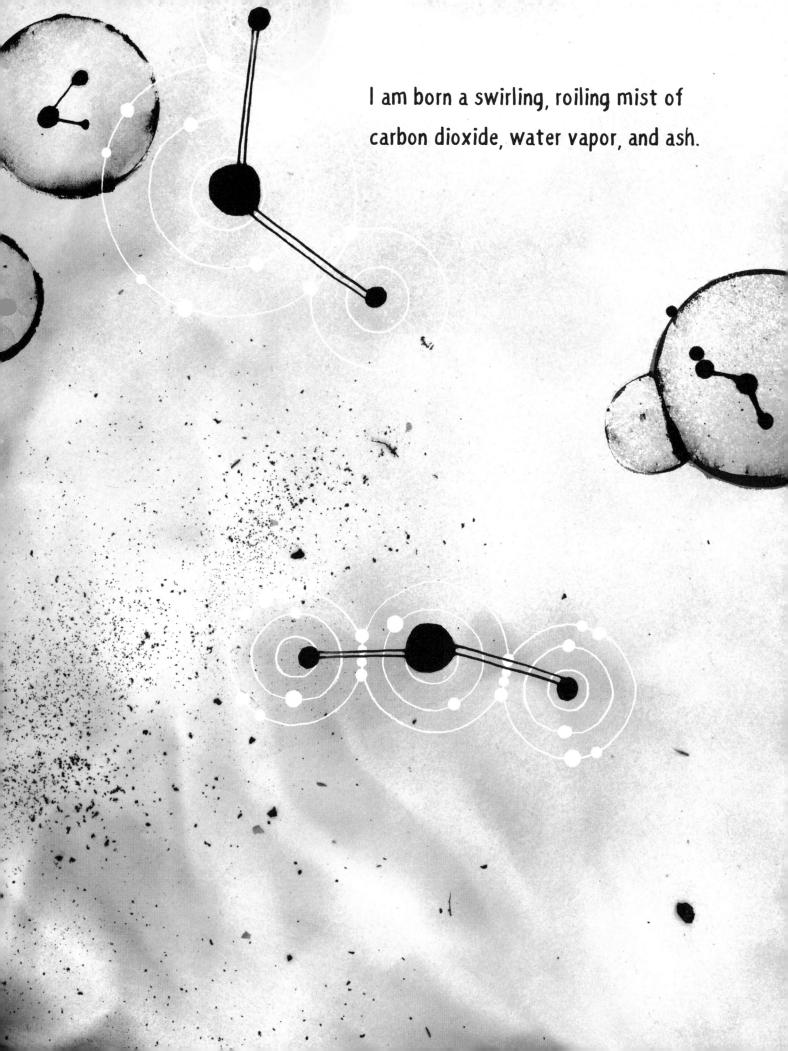

I am born a swirling, roiling mist of carbon dioxide, water vapor, and ash.

I am borne aloft in the heat's embrace,
soaring and spreading my wings.

I am smoke.

I am gentler than a feather, but I can cause harm. Even fearless firefighters dare not breathe me when battling flames.

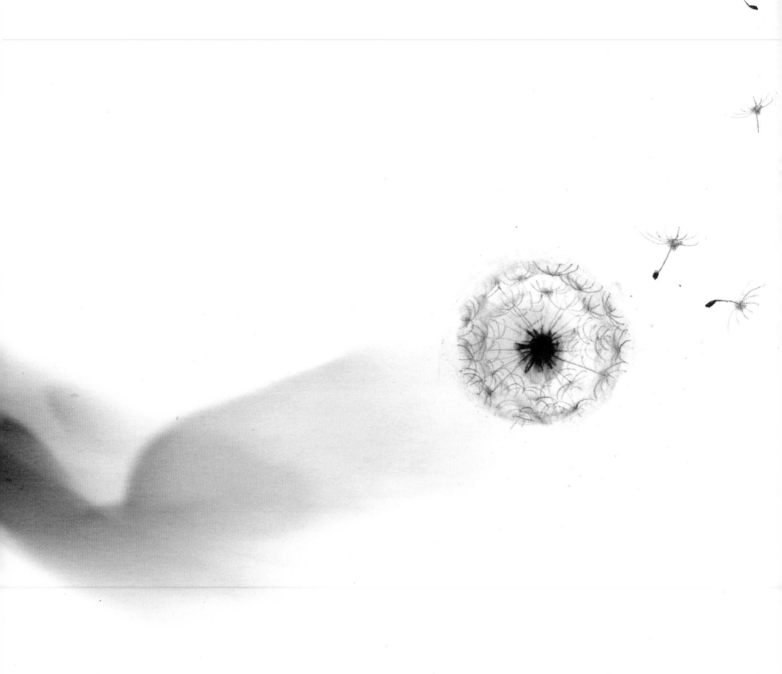

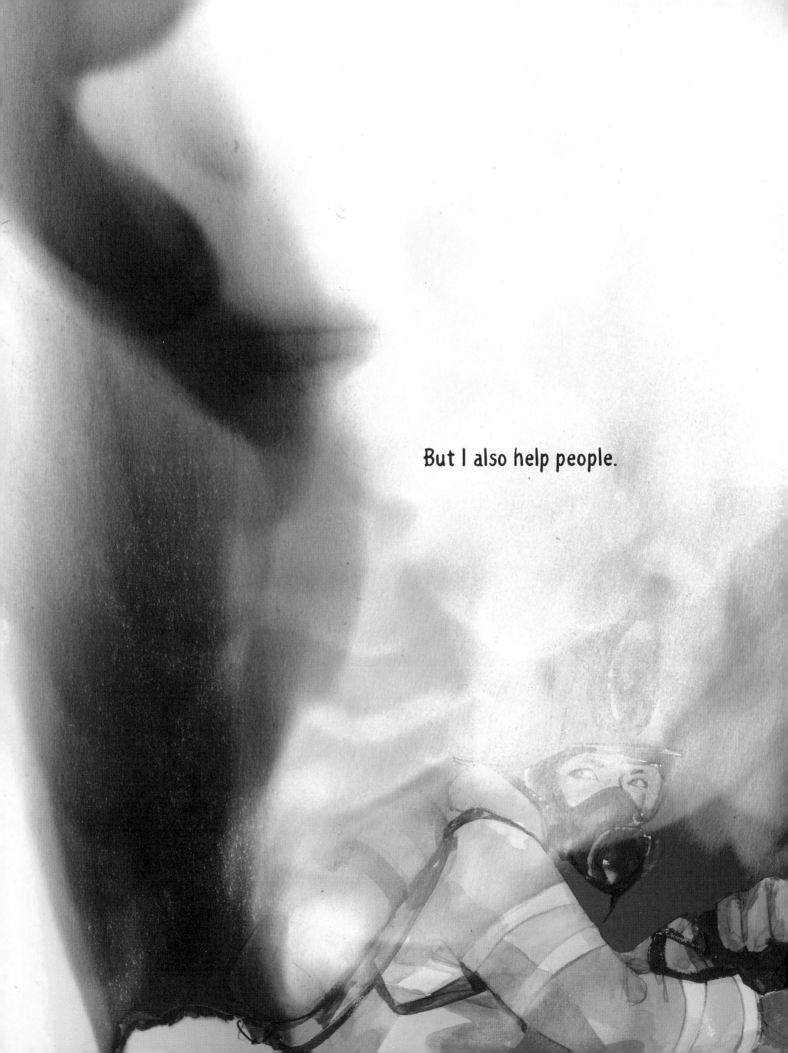

But I also help people.

I lack fingers, but I can nudge.

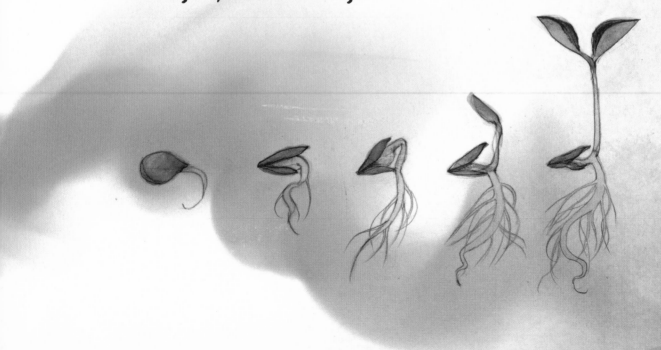

Hundreds of years ago, I helped Huron farmers coax pumpkin seeds to sprout with my warmth.

I lack hands, but I can push
out unwanted guests.

I helped ancient Greeks
drive termites, mosquitoes,
rodents, and other pests
from enclosed spaces.

I lack a mouth, but I can speak.

For centuries, I helped Chinese,
Native Americans of the Plains and
Southwest, and others signal one
another over long distances.

I lack a nose, but I can tickle others' noses.

Ancient Egyptians, Chinese, Babylonians, and people of
India burned incense to produce fragrant scents

I irritate eyes, but
I can soothe bees.

My smell beguiles guard bees so beekeepers can
harvest honey without disturbing them.

I cannot be sprinkled like salt, but I can flavor foods.

When I dance around meats, fish, or cheeses,
I cook, flavor, or preserve them.

I cannot kneel or bow, but I can participate in prayer.

I have attended Buddhist, Taoist, Shinto, Jewish, and Christian ceremonies for millennia.

I cannot touch, but I can help ease pain.

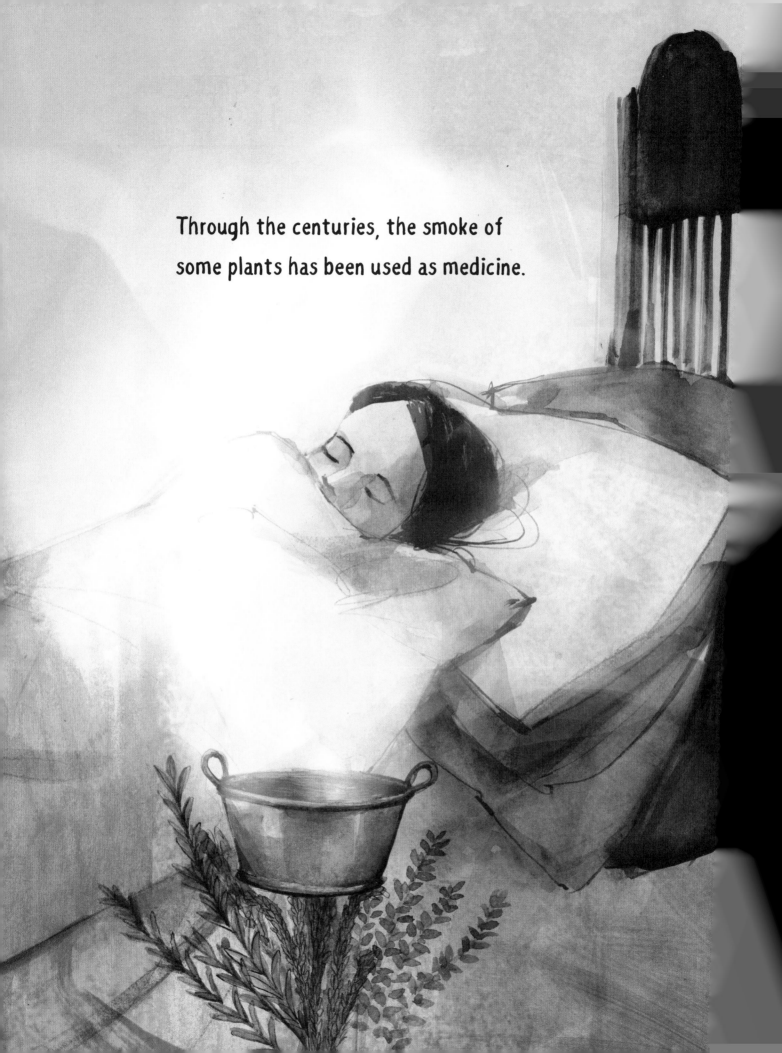

Through the centuries, the smoke of some plants has been used as medicine.

I rest at last. I float higher and higher, spread so thin I
cannot be seen. I ride the wind like a ship riding currents.

Eager leaves breathe
in my carbon dioxide.

My water vapor rains down.

Thirsty roots soak it up.

Plants transform me back into
wood. Tree trunks thicken.
Branches reach skyward.

I am patient.

Eventually, dead branches
fall to earth . . .

. . . to fuel another campfire.

I twirl again in dark dance.

I am smoke.

Smoke and Civilization

Everything changed when humans learned to make fire more than 1.6 million years ago. Fire kept frostbite, darkness, and night predators at bay. It helped make civilization possible. With fire came smoke, bestowing still more benefits on humankind. And fire and smoke have been blessings tempered by danger ever since.

Smoke speaks to us in this book, but its messages swirl and shift like smoke itself. The following notes—arranged by the first narrative line of the illustrated page—help to interpret its riddles.

I am born a swirling, roiling mist of carbon dioxide, water vapor, and ash . . .

Smoke billows upward as a gray, brown, or bluish cloud of gases and carbon particles (ash) from the burning of wood, coal, oil, or other organic matter. Much of the gas is carbon dioxide, which is called a greenhouse gas because it traps heat in the earth's atmosphere, just as the glass roof of a greenhouse traps heat beneath. Drifting in the ash near the top of this illustration is a molecule of water vapor, in which an oxygen atom shares electrons with two hydrogen atoms. Beneath that is a molecule of carbon dioxide, in which an atom of carbon shares electrons with two oxygen atoms.

The burning of fossil fuels since the dawn of the Industrial Revolution has flooded the atmosphere with carbon dioxide and other gases. The resultant overheating increases the power of storms, melts polar ice, raises sea levels, and causes more frequent and severe droughts. These effects—known as climate change—threaten wildlife, crops, and coastal cities. Replacing fossil fuels with solar, wind, hydro, tidal, and geothermal power is one way to reduce climate change. Planting trees is another, because trees remove carbon from the air and convert it to living tissue. Cutting down forests, especially in the tropics, leaves fewer trees to absorb carbon from the air.

Maybe smoke is trying to tell us these things in this book. But smoke won't let us forget the many ways it has helped us, too, since the dawn of civilization.

I lack fingers, but I can nudge . . .

The Huron people, also known as the Wyandot, are an Iroquoian-speaking Native American nation of the region north of Lake Ontario. A French missionary visiting the area in the 1630s reported seeing germination boxes filled with soil and pumpkin seeds suspended in the smoke above fires. This practice increased the number of seeds that sprouted, he reported. Huron women did most of the farming.

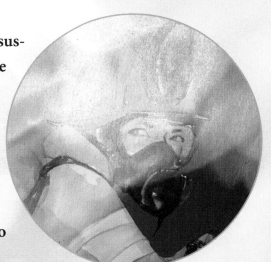

I lack hands, but I can push out unwanted guests ...

Fumigation means exposing enclosed spaces to smoke or fumes. Filling a building with smoke is a long-known way to drive out or kill pests.

I lack a mouth, but I can speak ...

Since 200 BCE (Before the Common Era), messages were sent along the Great Wall of China using smoke signals. The Chinese character for danger is shown in the illustration. In Greece, smoke signals for each letter of the alphabet were used as early as 150 BCE. The Greek letters in the illustration spell out the word "help."

Famed American explorers Meriwether Lewis and William Clark reported seeing North American Indigenous Plains people use smoke signals in 1805. Native Australians used smoke signals to announce their entry into new areas of the Western Desert.

Smoke (called *fumata*) is used at the Vatican in Rome during the selection of a pope. White smoke from the roof of the Sistine Chapel means that a new pope has been chosen. Black smoke indicates that the cardinals have failed to elect a pope in their latest round of voting.

I lack a nose, but I can tickle others' noses ...

The word "incense" comes from the Latin *incendere*, meaning "to burn." Ancient Egyptians burned incense to sweeten the smell of human homes. The illustration shows the huge, silver-plated Botafumeiro thurible swinging in contemporary times from the ceiling of the Cathedral of Santiago de Compostela in Spain. Its burning incense helps mask the odor of many worshippers crowded together.

I irritate eyes, but I can soothe bees ...

Beekeepers have known since ancient times that smoke calms bees, but only recently have scientists determined why. When startled, guard bees release a chemical scent to alert the hive, but smoke masks that scent so beekeepers can do their work without upsetting the bees.

I cannot be sprinkled like salt, but I can flavor foods . . .

Hanging food above burning or smoldering wood exposes the food to smoke. Smoke has been used around the world for centuries to flavor, cook, and preserve meats, fish, cheese, and other foods. Soaking food in salt water before smoking it further lengthens its preservation.

I cannot kneel or bow, but I can participate in prayer . . .

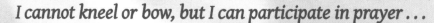

Clockwise from top left, the illustration shows a statue of Buddha, Catholic altar boys, a Jewish high priest at an incense altar, a Jewish menorah, a Babylonian priest with an incense burner, a Buddhist altar, and incense sticks in a Taoist temple.

Incense was used by ancient Babylonians in prayer, and it is estimated that the Chinese began using incense during worship around 2000 BCE. The use of incense is mentioned in the Book of Exodus (the second book of the Old Testament) and was part of Jewish Temple worship as long ago as 1200 BCE.

I cannot touch, but I can help ease pain . . .

The Greek physician Hippocrates, born around 460 BCE, recommended burning willow leaves to promote women's health. Fumigation and pipe smoking have been part of the Ayurvedic medicine practiced in India for more than 2,000 years. Native Americans used tobacco smoke as part of their medicine, and in the eighteenth century this practice spread to European countries. Now we understand the health hazards of tobacco smoke, one more danger hidden among smoke's benefits.

Sources

Baur, Fred, *Insect Management for Food Storage and Processing*. American Assn. of Cereal Chemists, 1984: 162–165.

Haynes, Sterling, M.D., "Special feature: Tobacco smoke enemas," *British Columbia Medical Journal* (December 2012): 496–497.

Herrera, Matthew, *Holy Smoke: The Use of Incense in the Catholic Church*. San Luis Obispo: Tixlini Scriptorium, 2012.

Jefferson, Lara, Marcello Pennachio, and Kayri Havens-Young, *Ecology of Plant-Derived Smoke: Its Use in Seed Germination*. Oxford University Press, 2014.

Journals of the Lewis and Clark Expedition. University of Nebraska Lincoln, https://lewisandclark-journals.unl.edu/item/lc.jrn.1805-07-20.

Leemans, W.F., *Foreign Trade in the Old Babylonian Period: As revealed by texts from southern Mesopotamia*. E.J. Brill, 1960.

Lis-Balchin, Maria, *Aromatherapy Science: A Guide for Healthcare Professionals*. Pharmaceutical Press, 2006.

Luhr Jensen smokehouse brochure.

Manohar, P. Ram, "Smoking and Ayurvedic Medicine in India." *Smoke: A Global History of Smoking*. Reaktion Books, 2004: 68–75.

Martyr, Philippa, "Hippocrates and Willow Bark? What you know about the history of aspirin is probably wrong," *The Conversation*, 10/18/20. https://theconversation.com/hippocrates-and-willow-bark-what-you-know-about-the-history-of-aspirin-is-probably-wrong-148087.

Mashable, "Evolution of Communication." http://mashable.com/2014/12/05/evolution-of-communication-brandspeak/#z6DksViOQOqB.

McGee, Harold, "Wood Smoke and Charred Wood." *On Food and Cooking* (rev. ed.). Scribner, 2004.

Myers, Fred, *Pintupi Country, Pintupi Self: Sentiment, Place, and Politics among Western Desert Aborigines*. University of California Press, 1991.

Neusner, Jacob, *The Talmud of Babylonia: Tractate Yoma*. Scholars Press, 1994.

United States Conference of Catholic Bishops, http://www.usccb.org/about/leadership/holy-see/francis/how-is-a-new-pope-chosen.cfm.

Visscher, P. Kirk, Richard S. Vetter, and Gene E. Robinson, Gene E., "Alarm pheromone perception in honeybees is decreased by smoke *(Hymenoptera: Apidae)*." *Journal of Insect Behavior* 8, 1 (January 1995): 11–18.

To create this book's illustrations, Mercè López captured patterns of swirling smoke on art paper suspended over smoky candle flames. She then deepened and elaborated the smoke impressions with watercolors and Photoshop finishes. With this unique method, she "let the smoke decide how the idea I had in mind would dance with it, giving freedom to the images."

The author, illustrator, and publisher offer grateful thanks to Stacey Parshall Jensen (sensitivity reader, diversity editor, and cultural consultant) and James Bird (screenwriter and author of The Brave*) for their insightful reviews of the text and illustrations.*

Henry Herz has authored ten picture books. His children's short stories have been published in *Highlights for Children, Ladybug Magazine,* and in anthologies for Albert Whitman & Company and Blackstone Publishing. Henry also writes adult science fiction and fantasy short stories. He holds a BS in Engineering from Cornell, an MS in Engineering from George Washington University, and an MA in Political Science from Georgetown. You can visit him at www.henryherz.com.

Mercè López graduated from Llotja Art School in Barcelona, Spain, and has illustrated for design, theater, and film as well as twenty children's books for Spanish and international book publishers. Her 2019 title *Lion of the Sky: Haiku for All Seasons* by Laura Purdie Salas received multiple starred reviews and was named a Center for Children's Books Gryphon Honor Book, an NCTE Notable Poetry Book, a *Kirkus* Best Picture Book, and a *Parents* Magazine Best Kids' Book.

Text © 2021 by Henry Herz • Illustrations © 2021 by Mercè López

Hardcover ISBN 978-0-88448-788-3

10 9 8 7 6 5 4 3 2 1

Tilbury House Publishers • Thomaston, Maine
www.tilburyhouse.com

Library of Congress Control Number: 2021938217

Designed by Frame25 Productions
Printed in Korea